Power and Empowerment

:+ Hei

Production

Power and Empowerment cover, book design
and implementation by Christopher Wilson at Oberphones
Illustrations by Jo@Kja-artists
Printed in the UK by CLOC

City & Guilds

1 Giltspur Street
London EC1A 9DD
T +44 (0)844 543 0000
publishingfeedback@cityandguilds.com
www.cityandguilds.com

Contents

Introduction

The idea of this Pocket Guide is to provide a quick and easy reference guide for care staff. The book is structured around three core questions:

- ▸ **WHAT** do we mean by power and empowerment?
- ▸ **WHY** is empowerment so important in social care?
- ▸ **HOW** can social care workers put empowerment into practice?

The standards of current qualifications in care have been carefully considered in writing this Pocket Guide.

WHAT do we mean by power and empowerment ?

Power and empowerment are regularly referred to in social care practice, and a clear understanding of these concepts is required for it to be effective. The need for an in-depth understanding of them is quite rightly reflected in qualification standards in the sector. However, many workers feel that these concepts are ambiguous and require clarification. This section therefore explores the following questions:

- ▶ **What is power?**
- ▶ **How is power constructed?**
- ▶ **What is powerlessness?**
- ▶ **What is empowerment?**

DEFINING POWER

Defining power is a complex task. It is worth beginning, therefore, at a simplistic level by considering dictionary definitions of power, which indicate that power is:

- An energy or force
- The possession of qualities (especially mental qualities) or strengths which are required to do something or get something done
- A legal authority to act (where aspects of choice may be removed from other people, eg when a crime has been committed, the state has the power to imprison someone)
- Political, financial or social force or influence
- The capacity of a system or machine to operate

In terms of social care, the following definitions of power are useful:

> *Power is the capacity to affect the behaviour of another – to persuade another to do something that he (sic) would not do on his own. Power is both purpose-driven and leadership-driven in whatever social setting it is applied.*
> **Tuitt** 2010

> *Power may comprise anything that establishes and maintains the control of people over other people. It applies in all social relationships.*
> **Morgenthau** 1978:8

> *Power is the production of causal effects. It is the bringing about of consequences.*
> **Lukes** 1986:6

HOW IS POWER CONSTRUCTED?

The construction of power is a term in common use in social care. The idea is that power is built up by a number of layers or aspects. This can be represented as follows:

▶ Dimensions
_____

▶ Realms
_____

▶ Forms
_____

▶ Faces
_____

▶ Sources
_____

DIMENSIONS OF POWER: POWER OVER, OF AND TO

Dominelli (2002:17) refers to French's 1985 definition of three dimensions of power: power over, power of and power to.

Power over refers to the power held by one dominant group over another. This could refer to the relative social power of certain groups or it could relate to the power of workers over service users.

Power of refers to the collective strength which people hold to make changes; it occurs when people come together for such a specific reason or purpose.

Power to refers to people's ability to make changes or decisions (also called 'transformative power'). This relates to either individuals or groups.

REFLECTING ON POWER

What do we have the power to do as individuals in our own lives?

▶ The power to make decisions
▶ The power to have a holiday
▶ The power to move house and live where we want to
▶ The power to build relationships with others
▶ The power to resist oppression and to be heard
▶ The power to manage our own finances
▶ The power to help ourselves
▶ The power to live each day as we want to

How do we promote this power in those with whom we work?

DIMENSIONS OF POWER: POWER WITH, TO AND WITHIN

Veneklasen and Miller of Just Associates (see, for example, 2006) have developed the idea of three positive forms of power, into which attempts at empowerment need to tap:

Power with

This refers to people finding common ground to build collective strength. It requires acknowledging diversity and disagreement while seeking common ground around values and actions.

Power to

This recognises the potential of each individual to shape their own life and their own world. It is a concept based on the idea that everyone has the power to make a difference, which can be maximised through individual learning and development.

Power within

This relates to a person's self-worth, self-knowledge and self-esteem. It relies on people having the ability to imagine something differently and to have hope. Spirituality, critical reflection and creative arts can all affirm power within.

Empowerment involves supporting people to develop all three forms of power.

REALMS OF POWER: PUBLIC, PRIVATE AND INTIMATE

In considering power as it relates to gender, **Veneklasen and Miller** (2002) identify the following three realms of power:

Public realm of power

This is visible power seen in employment and public life (where, for example, it is clear from an analysis of gender relations and the widely recognised gender pay gap that men and women are treated differently).

Private realm of power

This is the power which is expressed within people's private lives, such as in family relationships, friendships and intimate relationships.

Intimate realm of power

This is closely linked to the concept of power within; it relates to aspects of self-esteem, confidence and a person's relationship to their body.

FORMS OF POWER: SOFT POWER AND HARD POWER

This concept is drawn from politics and the writings of **Joseph Nye** (for example 2004). Despite the fact that its roots lie in the political arena, it is a useful concept for understanding forms of power and could be helpful in health and social care.

Hard power
This is about getting people to change their position and it relies on either inducements (carrots) or threats (sticks).

Soft power
This rests on the ability to shape the preferences of others. According to Nye, it is about leading people and modelling what you want them to do. It co-opts people rather than coercing them and is often seen as being based on the ability to get what you want through attraction.

FACES OF POWER

Various writers have developed the concept of three different faces of power (eg **Veneklasen and Miller** 2002, **Hinson and Healey** 2003, and **Lukes** 2004):

Hidden power

This is the power which is exercised 'behind the scenes', away from the public eye. Essentially, it is about agenda setting (relating to the terminology of the 'hidden agenda'). It is reflected in the fact that powerful people, powerful groups and powerful institutions maintain their influence by controlling what gets on the agenda.

Visible power

This is the power that we see; it is essentially about decision-making and is reflected in rules, structures and institutions.

Invisible power

This is seen as the most insidious of the three faces of power. It refers to the way powerful groups can influence the way people think (shaping beliefs, people's sense of self, etc) through processes of socialisation and internalisation. This is well explained by **Hinson and Healey** (2003:5):

When those who have the power to name and to socially construct reality choose not to see you or hear you [...] when someone with the authority, of a teacher, say, describes the world and you are not in it, there is a moment of psychic disequilibrium, as if you looked in the mirror and saw nothing. It takes some strength of soul – and not just individual strength but collective understanding – to resist this void, this non-being, into which you are thrust, and to stand up, demanding to be seen and heard.

SOURCES OF POWER

In a 1959 study which is now seen as a classic, **French and Raven** identified five sources or types of power:

Legitimate or positional power

The power that exists because of the way an organisation is structured or through how society is ordered. People have power because of their position within an organisation – for example, a manager can decide if a person is eligible for a service, and a police officer has the power to arrest someone.

Expert or professional power

Where a person is seen as having a bank of knowledge or expertise. Workers have expert power based on their professional training, qualifications and experience.

Reward power

The power gained through the ability to give 'rewards' of some kind. In social care, care staff have significant reward power, even if it means simply being attentive to service users.

> *Too often we underestimate the power of a touch, a smile, a kind word, a listening ear, an honest compliment, or the smallest act of caring, all of which have the potential to turn a life around.*
> **Leo Buscaglia** 1972

Referent power

The power created by the admiration and respect one person can have for another. This can be based on individual characteristics (or charisma) or on the admiration that people have for individuals from a particular profession. A good example of this is a person's respect for their GP (although GPs' power is also derived from legitimate and expert power).

Coercive power

The power based on the ability to apply punishment or sanctions. This power is most keenly felt in children's services (going to court for a care order) and mental health services (around the use of the Mental Health Act). The service user could be conscious of this power even if it has not been actively applied by workers. Coercive power can be seen as the most obvious and is perhaps the form of power which is most likely to build resentment or defensiveness from those on the receiving end of it.

The Inner London Probation Service (1993) recognised French and Raven's sources of power, but added two additional ones:

Societal power

The power based on the ideology of superiority. Some people experience oppression at the hands of others. Oppressors are powerful and oppressed people are less powerful. For example, an older person who experiences ageism is less powerful than a younger person.

The power to determine

In many ways, this is simply the power to make decisions which determine outcomes for another person. Workers can have the power to determine in a number of ways, such as in making decisions about actions to be taken.

DEFINING POWERLESSNESS

> *A sensation of being out of control with no apparent solution to help regain control*
> *Complete lack of control, authority or status to affect how others will treat or act towards you*
> *Lack of strength, competence or skills to overcome realities in life that have no current apparent solution.*
> **LiveStrong** 2011

Although obvious, powerlessness is best defined as the absence of power and control in your own life. People often feel a lack of power, influence, strength or ability around choices in their own life, the difficulties they face and the means to resolve these.
Maclean and Harrison 2010

Powerlessness within services

Some service users can maintain some power over their own life, possibly because they are articulate or have active family support or make full use of direct payments, etc.

Many more service users experience a significant sense of powerlessness. The service user is likely to have been through significant changes in their life, most of which were unwanted. They may have acquired a disability or mental health problem, or may have been subjected to abuse. Having contact with services can be difficult for some people to adjust to. If the service user has had to move into a care home then this can be a profound change. Often the decisions the service user is still able to make are relatively minor and they have little real say over key decisions. The service user didn't plan or want to develop mental health problems or to acquire a disability, which can result in them having a profound sense of powerlessness.

The attitude of workers, the way services are organised and their ethos can all influence whether this sense of powerlessness is heightened or reduced. Many service users feel powerless and their lack of confidence (due to the knocks of life) is likely to result in a sense that they are unable to change their life in the way they would like to. If the service user develops the view that they cannot change anything because they are powerless this is termed 'learned helplessness'.

Following changes in the delivery of health and social care in recent years, people may feel that they do now have a voice, either in terms of being able to express their needs to providers of services or to speak out if they feel that service provision is not meeting their needs. The role of advocacy, including independent advocacy services, will be explored later in this Guide.

Why might the following people feel their power is limited?

► Service users
► Family members
► Partners and other informal or unpaid carers
► Social care workers
► Service managers

FACTORS WHICH RESTRICT PEOPLE'S SENSE OF THEIR OWN POWER

- ▶ Communication differences
- ▶ Prejudice
- ▶ Real or perceived stereotyping
- ▶ Being in a crisis and feeling like things are getting too much to cope with
- ▶ Ill health or disability
- ▶ Trauma, abuse or neglect
- ▶ Financial concerns
- ▶ Access to resources and the inaccessibility of services or opportunities (for any reason)
- ▶ Oppression
- ▶ The impact of significant life events such as loss or bereavement

DEFINING EMPOWERMENT

The process by which individuals and groups gain power, access to resources and control over their own lives. In doing so, they gain the ability to achieve the highest personal and collective aspirations and goals.
   Robbins, Chatterjee and Canda 1998:91

The process of helping individuals, families, groups and communities to increase their personal, interpersonal, socio-economic and political strength to develop influence toward improving their circumstances.
   Barker 2009

Intimately connected with individual's feelings of self-worth and self-confidence and sense of efficacy [...] is also inseparably linked to the social and political conditions in which people live.
   Kreisberg 1992:19

FREIRE

The Brazilian educator **Paulo Freire** is well known for his writings on empowerment. His book *The Pedagogy of the Oppressed*, first published in English in 1970, is seen as a seminal text. Freire saw empowerment as being created rather than being 'given'. He viewed empowerment as:

- Power in learning being shared between individuals
- A means and an outcome in itself
- Liberating for individuals
- Leading to a 'collective critical consciousness' (ie groups of people criticise an institutionalised perspective on what education involves and work together to adapt and improve this)
- Focused on social change through collective action

The imagery and language employed to talk about power revolve around construction. This is perhaps very fitting, as feeling disempowered can resemble feeling as if there were an insurmountable brick wall ahead of you.

Social care work literature often refers to a 'toolbox' of skills. Empowerment begins by understanding how the brick wall of exclusion is constructed, so that the social care worker can make use of their skills to 'deconstruct' the brick wall.

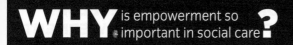

WHY is empowerment so important in social care **?**

Smith (2010) asserts that a 'clear understanding of and strategy for dealing with power and its consequences are important components of the practitioner's toolkit'.

This section should help you to identify why power and empowerment are such key issues in health and social care practice by exploring the following questions:

▶   **Why do social care workers need to develop their understanding of power and empowerment?**

▶   **What are the benefits of empowerment?**

▶   **Why do social care workers find empowerment challenging?**

WHY DO SOCIAL CARE WORKERS NEED TO DEVELOP THEIR UNDERSTANDING OF POWER AND EMPOWERMENT?

- ► Power is always an issue for health and social care workers
- ► Empowerment requires a clear understanding of power dynamics and how disempowered service users can be
- ► Effective support for service users relies on practitioners having a well-developed understanding of power and empowerment
- ► Social care workers may well misunderstand power and empowerment
- ► Contemporary policy and likely future changes to social care are based on issues of power and empowerment
- ► Safeguarding is a central role for social care workers, and power and its misuse are key issues in safeguarding practice
- ► Empowerment lies at the heart of social care practice
- ► Social care practice can be disempowering, especially where practitioners lack awareness of power and empowerment
- ► Social care workers work with people who are disempowered

POWER DYNAMICS IN HELPING RELATIONSHIPS

Whenever one individual provides services for another, there is an immediate power relationship (and usually this power is imbalanced between the people in that relationship). In terms of how services work, the power relationship is influenced by the following factors:

Power held by the service user:

▶ The service or assessment is meant to be for the benefit of the service user

▶ The service user has the right to complain if they are not satisfied with the service provided

▶ The service user may have other people to turn to for support (eg family members, advocates or friends)

▶ The personal qualities of the service user can be a source of power (eg if they are articulate, confident, educated, etc)

The service user's perception of their own power may be undermined by:

► One or more negative experiences that have markedly reduced their confidence

► A profound sense of vulnerability due to the fact that they are dependent on the social care worker, which inhibits people from making complaints

► A lack of knowledge of their rights

► Isolation

► Previous attempts at claiming power over their own life have failed (learned helplessness)

► The person's ability to express themselves may be impaired by mental health issues or a learning disability

The social care worker will be powerful by comparison to the service user. Possible reasons for this could include:

- ▶ Age, gender or race of the worker compared to the service user (eg a thirty-year-old white woman supporting a black woman in her seventies)
- ▶ The worker has a role or a job to do; this is heightened if the worker presents himself/herself as being busy, having lots to do and not enough time to spend with the service user
- ▶ The service user needs care support, not the worker, and the worker knows a lot about the service user
- ▶ The worker is one of a team and has the power to influence the viewpoint of team colleagues through recording or team discussion

A social care worker's perception of the limits of their power may be influenced by:

▶ The worker's professional values which prompt them to show respect for the service user, recognise that service users are experts about their own situation, etc
▶ The knowledge that service users could complain about them
▶ Awareness of the presence of colleagues and regular supervision from their line manager

PRACTICE EXAMPLE

Thomas is 45 and has been a manager in a local engineering firm for several years. He recently had a stroke and is recovering well, but needed some support around basic household tasks on his discharge from hospital. He is divorced and his grown-up children are both living some way off whilst they are at university.

▶ How might it feel for Thomas having a professional come into his home for the first time in his life to offer him support?

▶ How would a social care professional ensure Thomas felt in control of the services he decided to access?

▶ What might make Thomas feel disempowered? And how might these issues be overcome?

POWER AND SOCIAL CARE SETTINGS

Foucault (1977:27) identified that power is everywhere and comes from everywhere. Since power is so pervasive in society, social care workers need to develop a clear understanding of what it is and its potential impact on the lives of service users and on their practice. As **Cooper** (2011:20) states:

> *Social care work is essentially about power [...] interventions into others' lives is an intervention into networks of power relationships. It is the structures of power and powerlessness that produce both the problems and the potential solutions.*

Practitioners do not always recognise the power issues in their work; they sometimes only reflect on power issues when they are explicit, missing the importance of power in every situation.

Having an understanding of the impact of power in practice could not be described in itself as empowerment, but it might be described as 'power sensitive' practice (**Gardner** 2011) and it is the first vital step towards empowerment.

Issues of power are real and embedded in practice and cannot be sidelined or treated as subordinate questions to be dealt with only if time permits.
> **Smith** 2010

Power is intrinsic to all social interaction – we cannot escape the significance of it in our dealings with people.
> **Thompson** 2001

CONTEMPORARY PRACTICE AND POLICY DEVELOPMENT

Contemporary social care practice has rejected the idea of the professional gift model of support and is working towards the concept of empowerment (**Social Platform** 2010:1).

In the early part of this century, the Labour Government developed what it referred to as the empowerment agenda. This led to what is often described as a 'frenetic period' of policy development in social care and other related sectors.

At the time of writing, the Coalition Government is promoting the idea of the Big Society, which they describe as based on community empowerment – in terms of the transfer of power from central government to local communities (**Chanan and Miller** 2010).

Concepts of self-directed care, self-assessment, co-production and personalisation are all part of contemporary practice and appear in the policy directions setting out visions for the future of social care.

The Scottish Government (2005) identify that understanding power and its fluid nature is vital in understanding the likely changes to social care and social work practice in the 21st century.

Change which is imposed and isn't well explained can lead to people feeling disempowered, and the pace of change in contemporary social care work can certainly lead to confusion. You may feel like you need a crystal ball to foresee change! At the very least, it is helpful to have a well-developed understanding of power and empowerment to anticipate likely changes to social care policy and the impact of these on practice.

SOCIAL CARE IS BUILT ON EMPOWERMENT

Understanding power dynamics and the impact that these have on people's lives arguably remain what sets social care apart from other professions. **Higham** (2005) states that one of the things which makes social care a unique profession is that it builds on an 'awareness of structural oppression, power, service users' rights and responsibilities and social inclusion'.

Social care is built around an understanding of human rights and how these must be respected in everyday life for all individuals. Empowerment and self-determination are fundamental human rights and therefore must be central to all social care practice.

It is clear, therefore, that power and empowerment are key issues in social care practice. Since we refer regularly to the 'construction' of power, it is fitting to talk about social care work being built on empowerment.

SOCIAL CARE SUPPORTS PEOPLE WHO ARE DISEMPOWERED

Hepworth et al (2010:14) highlight the fact that social care professionals work with '... individuals, groups and entire communities who lack the power of self-determination ...' They go on to explain that 'indeed the powerless are more likely to have government agencies and public policy exert significant authority in their lives.'

This can lead to a vicious cycle where the more disempowered people are, the more others exert their power.

Fook (2002:51) suggests that people can often be disempowered by the 'best intentions' of professionals. Sometimes, doing too much for someone can lead to the 'learned helplessness' effect occurring, to dependencies being created and to workers' own needs to be the 'helper' being catered for, as opposed to the service users' need to be in control of their own life.

If social care workers do not have a well developed understanding of power, powerlessness and empowerment, not only are they unlikely to be able to support service users effectively, but they may also further disempower service users who are already powerless.

SAFEGUARDING AND EMPOWERMENT

Safeguarding is a central component of social care in every field of practice. In order to safeguard people, social care workers must have a clear understanding of power.

Power and abuse are linked in many ways.

- Abuse involves a misuse of power. For example, the **NSPCC** (2011) highlight the fact that 'child abuse [...] is an abuse of power'
- Many victims of abuse are in some kind of relationship with their abuser which involves a power dynamic
- Social care workers can feel powerless in their work to prevent abuse

The **Duluth** model of domestic violence (online 2011), which has been developed since the early 1980s, highlights the way that power and control are central to domestic violence.

Physical/sexual violence

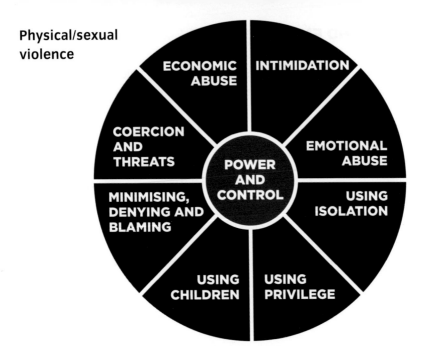

ECONOMIC ABUSE

INTIMIDATION

COERCION AND THREATS

EMOTIONAL ABUSE

POWER AND CONTROL

USING ISOLATION

MINIMISING, DENYING AND BLAMING

USING CHILDREN

USING PRIVILEGE

It is now widely recognised that since power and abuse are so inextricably linked, empowering people can be an effective method of safeguarding. For example:

- ▶ **White et al** (2003) identified empowerment as a key component to safeguarding adults in residential care from abuse and exploitation
- ▶ **The Department of Health** (2009) found that in terms of adult safeguarding, empowerment is a protective factor against abuse and identified evidence that shifting the power balance within families and between service users and professionals can have very positive safeguarding outcomes
- ▶ **Warrin** (2010) claims that the effective integration of safeguarding and empowerment contains the 'seeds for a transformation of care' with regard to the prevention of abuse and neglect
- ▶ **The CSCI** (2008) sees empowering individuals as a crucial factor in safeguarding

WHAT ARE THE BENEFITS OF EMPOWERMENT?

Croft and Beresford (1992) assert that empowerment creates mutual respect between practitioners and the users of services; it certainly has major benefits for both.

The benefits to service users are:

▶ Raises self-esteem

▶ Enables people to mobilise their own resources

▶ Reduces isolation

▶ Reduces risk and the likelihood of abuse occurring

▶ Makes the person feel that professionals are working with them as opposed to 'doing to' them

▶ Reduces the potential creation of dependency on services and professionals, and 'learned helplessness'

The benefits to practitioners are:

- Provides a very practical focus or 'recipe' for practice
- Leads to increased job satisfaction
- Enables better assessment and planning to take place
- Ensures the outcomes of work with people can be monitored and shared more accurately
- Can enable new services to be developed around people's own view of their needs
- Can reduce potential risk to people and isolation of individuals
- Enables workers to learn from each other's practices and develop an evidence base for good practice
- It can improve relationships with and between the people you support, thus ensuring people are happier and more settled

WHY DO SOCIAL CARE WORKERS FIND EMPOWERMENT CHALLENGING?

Despite the fact that empowerment is an essential component of social care practice, practitioners can be challenged by it. The reasons for this include:

▶ Lack of understanding of power and empowerment
▶ Reluctance to 'own' their own power
▶ Lack of understanding of theories of power
▶ Resource limitations
▶ Managerialist approaches

MANAGERIALIST APPROACHES

Managerialism and empowerment are closely linked, in two main ways.

Managerialism is about a shift in power

Clarke et al (2000) define managerialism as an approach which disregards professionalism and undermines localised democracy by placing the power firmly in the hands of central government. Whilst Governments argue that current policy focuses on devolving power, the setting of performance targets and progress measurement does place power in the hands of central government.

Managerialism constrains empowerment

Smith (2010) asserts that managerialist practice constrains workers from fully using an empowerment focus. The procedural focus of contemporary practice certainly makes empowerment much more challenging for practitioners.

THE MUNRO REVIEW

Professor Eileen Munro's 2011 review into child protection services highlights the impact of managerialist approaches on workers and users of services, and in particular how excessive bureaucracy can paralyse professional practice, which in turn reduces empowerment.

Munro (2011 online: 132–133) states that the level of:

[...] prescription has not been helpful, resulting in a degree of bureaucratisation that has unintentionally distracted from key aspects of practice by absorbing too much professional time. As the system's dependency on rules and prescription has grown, there has been insufficient freedom and confidence in the exercise of professional judgement. There has also been a worrying change in the priority afforded to building strong relationships with children, young people and families, and working directly with them [...] The prescription of how to practice has sapped the profession's ability to develop

its own knowledge and skills base. Most worryingly, there has been so much focus on improving social work skill in the timely assessment of children and families, that insufficient attention has been given to providing social workers with the knowledge and skills to help them.

This is equally relevant in the context of social care, where a similar impact can be witnessed from managerialist approaches. This is seen by Munro in terms of the vicious cycles which occur from:

- Higher referral rates and levels of need experienced by people in times of crisis
- More paperwork = less time with users of services
- Staff anxiety resulting in stress
- Increased sickness rates
- Increased caseloads for the workers who remain

RESOURCE LIMITATIONS

Resources are always finite, but over recent years resource limitations have had an increasing impact on social care provision (see, for example, **Walker and Beckett** 2003, **Betts Adams, Matto and LeCroy** 2009 and **Zastrow** 2010).

As **Rodgers** (2003:93) asserts, 'Power is scarce, unequal and often coercive, which tends to lead to conflict over access to finite resources.' The current financial climate within which we operate will have an impact on power and empowerment in various ways.

The International Federation of Social Workers (2011) highlights that the recent economic downturn has had a major impact on the availability of resources and services at a time when more people are actually in need of support.

There is a fundamental debate at the heart of this around people's rights and how the state should serve to meet their needs at times of crisis. People may feel that they have the right to a certain service or level of support, but thresholds for services can change at times of scarce resources. This might mean that something to which they could have been entitled last year is no longer there or that they are now seen as having a level of need which means this service is no longer available to them. Changes to benefit entitlements are a good example of this.

THOUGHT BOX

▶ *What has been the impact of financial restraints in your field of practice?*

▶ *Do you think this has led service users to feel disempowered?*

▶ *How have/could you address this disempowerment in your work with individuals or groups of people?*

LACK OF UNDERSTANDING OF POWER AND EMPOWERMENT

Power is an incredibly complex concept, which can lead to either misunderstandings or adopting a simplistic view which misses a number of key issues. There are a number of common misunderstandings around power in social care.

Power is viewed as the same for everyone

Different people, groups, cultures and individuals (including within the social care profession) have different understandings of what power is, what equality and inequality means and therefore what needs to occur to address this. This can lead to misunderstanding of the nature of people's issues and disempowerment, which leads to our values and cultural norms being imposed upon those we seek to empower. Recognising and celebrating diversity is therefore a key aspect of empowerment practice, as is understanding your own definitions of power.

Power is seen as wholly negative

Power is very often negatively viewed by social care workers. This may be because social care workers so often see and work with the consequences of abuse and significant misuse of power. It might also be based on a misunderstanding of empowerment and some workers wrongly feeling that they should not have power. It is important to remember that:

Nothing is innately wrong with the word power, but it has commonly been used in contexts that have given it monstrous connotations. To many people, power conjures visions of autocracy [...] many think of power in terms of brute force, cunning, hatred and injustice.

Shivers 2001:133

Power can in fact be used to achieve positive change and it is vital that both the negative and positive sides of power are recognised by social care workers. Where power is viewed entirely negatively, practitioners will not be comfortable about their power – which is an essential aspect of empowerment.

Power is understood simply as a commodity

As we have already seen, there is considerable debate about whether power is an attribute, capacity or commodity (eg **Bernhagen** 2003). **Fook** (2002:48) suggests that, in social care, power has traditionally been understood as a commodity, meaning that:

▶ Power is viewed as something which workers possess
▶ Power is viewed as being transferred from one person to another
▶ If the worker transfers power to service users, this leaves the worker as the person who is disempowered
▶ There is a limited quantity of power which means that we have to make choices about who to empower and base these choices on who we feel is most disadvantaged by their lack of power

It is important that practitioners develop their awareness of power and recognise that it is much more than a simple commodity.

DENIAL OF POWER

Often social care workers struggle to identify their power and identify how powerless they feel.

There may be a number of reasons for this:

- ▶ Managerialist approaches to practice can leave practitioners feeling powerless
- ▶ Social care workers may feel uncomfortable with owning power and so internalise a denial of power
- ▶ Empowerment may have been misunderstood, so that some workers feel they should not talk about the power they own
- ▶ Power is often negatively viewed by practitioners who then feel less able to articulate the power they have

The more power that social care workers have, the less they seem ready or able to own that power.

Ironically, often the people best able to identify power, the way it operates and the impact it has, are those who are powerless.
ILPS 1993

Understanding why empowerment is important and what the challenges might be are key to practice implementation. This section of the Pocket Guide has highlighted the fact that there are many reasons why empowerment is important to effective health and social care practice. However, perhaps the most important reason of all is that:

Where practitioners lack an understanding of power and empowerment, service users are left more vulnerable to abuse.
Association of Directors of Social Services 2005

HOW can social care workers put empowerment into practice?

The Pocket Guide '**WHAT? WHY? HOW?**' format is probably more important for this subject than any other since it is impossible to *do* the '**HOW**' (empowering practice) unless you understand the '**WHAT**' (how power is constructed) and the '**WHY**' (why people are disempowered). This section explores the main components of empowerment by considering the following questions:

▶ **Is empowerment aspirational or achievable?**

▶ **What are the key components of empowerment?**

▶ **How can social care workers apply the concept of empowerment to their practice?**

EMPOWERMENT: ASPIRATION OR REALITY?

As the **WHY?** section of this Pocket Guide explored, the barriers to empowerment can mean that empowerment is challenging for workers. As a result, **Gardner** (2011) asserts that it may be better to see empowerment as an 'aspirational rather than attainable goal'.

Whilst Gardner's view is understandable, it is important to recognise that there are aspects of empowerment which are attainable in contemporary social care practice.

Many writers describe theories as 'recipes' for practice (see, for example, **Lopez** 2011). In considering theories and models then, it can be useful to take the 'ingredients' into account.

Empowerment can be seen as an abstract concept. Viewing empowerment as a recipe and considering the key ingredients can make it more concrete and therefore assist practitioners in working in an empowering way.

The best cooks adapt recipes taking into account the ingredients they have at hand so that the dish they produce will turn out differently each time. Empowerment can be used in practice whatever the limitations are, where the concept is broken down into its components (or ingredients). In this way, a social care worker committed to empowerment can put the key components into practice, whatever challenges they face, by adapting the 'recipe' – taking into account the ingredients and equipment available and the unique nature of each service user's situation.

KEY COMPONENTS OF EMPOWERMENT

Empowerment involves:

- Understanding the construction of power
- Seeing the service user as the expert
- Service users giving their consent in a fully informed way to all aspects of their assessment and service provision
- Owning power and using it responsibly
- Recognising power differentials
- Viewing problems as the way in which we develop resilience, as opposed to insurmountable difficulties
- Developing positive attitudes and practice
- Acknowledging the dignity of risk and managing risk proactively
- Encouraging hopefulness
- Facilitating user involvement
- Enabling and facilitating learning

- ▶ Listening and hearing
- ▶ Drawing on the strengths perspective
- ▶ Addressing inequality
- ▶ Assuming personal responsibility
- ▶ Rejecting the idea that problems develop because of personal inadequacy
- ▶ Connecting with others who have faced similar issues to then be able to achieve broader collective and social change
- ▶ Helping service users to develop resources
- ▶ Exchanging information

UNDERSTANDING THE CONSTRUCTION OF POWER

As can be seen from the **WHAT?** section of this Pocket Guide, power is a complex and dynamic concept. The first and perhaps most important step in empowerment is to understand the way that power is constructed and to be clear about what power means to you as an individual. A poorly developed understanding of power can certainly lead to an abuse of that power.

Understanding power as the starting point for empowerment is widely recognised. For example, **Bar-On** (2002) asserts that social care workers must increase their understanding of power and its dynamics if they are to effectively support those people that society excludes and makes vulnerable.

One of the issues in understanding power is that much of the way in which it is often defined in writings is based on a dichotomy of 'either/or'. **Fook** (2002:49) calls this 'binary oppositional relations'.

For example, workers with an underdeveloped understanding of the complexities of power may believe that:

► People are either powerful *or* powerless:
  ► Workers hold the power and therefore service users have none
  ► Some in society hold power because of their ethnicity, gender, sexuality, etc and others have less
  ► Managers hold the power in many social care settings around resources, and workers often feel powerless to do the work which brought them into the profession in the first place

- ▶ Power held by workers is either good *or* bad:
  - ▶ Good for society in keeping people safe; for the service user in having a system to turn to in times of stress or crisis; for the worker in having a basis for decision-making, etc
  - ▶ Bad for service users if their choices are restricted or if certain actions need to take place in order to keep a person safe; for workers in having to take actions which others perceive as negative, etc
- ▶ People need either care *or* control
- ▶ Expertise lies with either the practitioner *or* the service user

The concept of empowerment is based on the need for these notions to be harmonised, as opposed to them being set up as incompatible opposites to each other in these ways. It is therefore vital that social care practitioners recognise where they stand in terms of their understanding of power – how do they see power and how can they reconcile such opposing views so that they can work in an empowering way?

It is important to recognise that:

- People can be *both* powerful *and* powerless (in different situations, for example)
- Power can be *both* positive *and* negative – it is the way that power is used which makes it 'good' or 'bad'
- In some situations we may need a balance of *both* care *and* control
- Service users are the experts on their own life and their situation: however, professionals may have expertise on the process of finding solutions or on how to navigate services which service users may not have

OWNING POWER

Social care workers can be uncomfortable with power and often do not see themselves as powerful. However, in order to empower others, it is important to have power, and a vital part of this is recognising and owning power. **Alice Walker** (in Self Esteem Experts online) states that: 'The most common way people give up their power is by thinking they don't have any.'

The following poem demonstrates the need for each of us, as individuals, to own our power:

It is our light not our darkness that most frightens us
Our deepest fear is not that we are inadequate.
Our deepest fear is that we are powerful beyond measure.
It is our light not our darkness that most frightens us.
We ask ourselves, who am I to be brilliant, gorgeous,
*   talented and fabulous?*

Actually, who are you not to be?
You are a child of God.
Your playing small does not serve the world.
There's nothing enlightened about shrinking so that other
*   people won't feel insecure around you.*
We were born to make manifest the glory of
*   God that is within us.*
It's not just in some of us; it's in everyone.
And as we let our own light shine,
*   we unconsciously give other people*
*   permission to do the same.*
As we are liberated from our own fear,
Our presence automatically liberates others.

Marianne Williamson 1992

USING POWER RESPONSIBLY

Most professional workers have significant power compared to a service user. When a worker gives choices to a service user, they are applying their resource power. This is done through the worker deciding which choices they are going to make available to the person and through the manner of their presentation of these options.

Service users may pick up from workers what answer they feel the latter would like them to give and so comply with this.

We need to maximise service users' autonomy and so all workers need to be conscious of how they are using their power. Are workers using their power to enhance the service user's independent decision-making skills or to guide the service user to an option that is easy for the staff and the service to respond to?

THOUGHT BOX

▶ *What do you understand by responsible use of your own power?*

▶ *What do you do if you feel a colleague has not used their own power in a fully responsible fashion?*

In order to make responsible use of the power they have, it is vital that health and social care workers:

▶ Understand the nature of their power

▶ Reflect on their listening and communication skills, and the way in which they present themselves and the power they hold to the people with whom they work

▶ Seek to understand each person as a unique individual, recognising the factors which oppress them or which restrict their access to resources and opportunities

► Reflect on the choices they offer to service users, and the factors influencing their assessment and planning

► Explain their actions in a way which shows that their decision-making has been considerate, respectful, informed by knowledge and evidence, and therefore legitimate (sometimes referred to as defensible decision-making)

The problem with power is not power itself, it is how to achieve its responsible use.
Robert F Kennedy online undated

PRACTICE EXAMPLE

Shara is 14 and recently came into care. She is being cared for at a local children's home and since moving there, she has presented workers with some concerns about her behaviour. Shara is often tearful and reluctant to talk to workers, but she has gone missing on two occasions; it is suspected that she is self-harming, and her eating is irregular.

When workers try to talk to Shara, all she will say is that she hates it there and wants to go back to her family.

▶ What could Shara's keyworkers do to help her open up and settle in?

▶ What factors are making Shara feel disempowered?

▶ What practical ideas would you have to help empower Shara?

▶ What choices are available to Shara, and how could workers enable her to explore these to promote her independence and sense of control over her own life?

LANGUAGE AND POWER

Mooney et al (2011) make clear that language can be used to exercise power. Language creates barriers between people; it can disempower, dehumanise and ultimately depersonalise.

Depersonalisation: 'ic' is often added to a diagnosis to describe someone – diabetic, schizophrenic, etc. This is incredibly depersonalising. It is much more personalised and ultimately empowering to refer to someone as living with a diagnosis of diabetes rather than as 'a diabetic'.

Dehumanisation: the process of dehumanisation is about people not being seen as a valued human being or the worth of a person being reduced so that they are seen as not quite human (sub-human). Language in the health and social care field is often dehumanising. Perhaps the best example of this is the language used around personal care. For example, people generally 'eat' but as soon as someone comes into contact with social care services, they will be referred to as 'feeding themselves' or needing to be 'fed'. In other situations we only refer to feeding when talking about babies and animals. The central message received by people is that they are now less than human.

Many social care workers using traditional assessment forms use this language without a second thought. If you are honest, as a care worker how many times have you asked someone if they can feed themselves? Changing the language that we use as practitioners is a very practical first step in respecting people as unique individuals and seeking to empower them.

CARE AND CONTROL

With power comes responsibility. Social care and health services need to use the power they have in a responsible manner. The care and control debate has been one of the main arenas where professionals have considered: 'How do we use our power responsibly?'

Services need to enable service users to feel supported and valued. This can be hard to achieve, for example where an assessment is being completed around a person's access to a substance misuse treatment. The emphasis must be on services being offered in order to support the person to engage with services to reduce their substance use. However, part of the care side of the worker's role is shown by making clear to service users the possible consequences of their actions if they do not engage fully with services. Boundaries are important for all of us.

One of the most obvious areas where this debate takes place is around whether parents (and other significant adults) ought to be able to use physical punishment to control their children.

▶   What is your view of this issue?

▶   Do parents have the right to smack their own child?

▶   What is a smack and when is a smack too hard and unacceptable as a punishment?

▶   When does smacking become physical abuse, and how do you draw this line?

▶   Does society have the right to legislate on this issue – either to allow it or to ban parental smacking? Why, or why not?

Public opinion on this issue can be very strong, and the control of people's private behaviour by the state and the law is a hot topic. Can and should service users' behaviour be 'controlled' in certain ways?

SEEING SERVICE USERS AS EXPERTS

Seeing the service user as the expert on their own situation is a key aspect of a range of contemporary social care theories.

Think about how you would feel if a worker came to your home to provide you with some form of care. If they didn't acknowledge and respect your own knowledge of yourself, your culture, your view of your own needs and your choices about the care you require, would you let them back in your home again?

The strengths perspective includes this as a key component and an understanding of this concept can be very helpful in empowering people.

THE STRENGTHS PERSPECTIVE

The strengths perspective came about partly as a reaction against two features of traditional health and social care provision.

1. An increasing medical classification and diagnosis of individuals which leads to the labelling of large sections of society.
2. Assessments are weighted towards listing people's deficits, vulnerabilities and negative past experiences. In the current environment where demand for services is increasing but the resources available have been cut, there is an increased focus and heightening of service users' lack of capability and risks.

In both these suggestions, there is a structural or bureaucratic bias against recognising people's strengths, abilities and resilience. Professionals may be led to make use of a language that is pathologising and alienating in order to ensure that service users have access to services.

Saleebey (1996) generated the following comparison of professional pathologising against the strengths perspective.

Pathology	Strengths
Person is defined as a 'case'. Symptoms add up to a diagnosis	Person is defined as unique. Traits, talents and resources add up to strengths
Intervention is problem-focused	Intervention is possibility-focused
Service user accounts are filtered by a professional to aid the generation of a diagnosis	Personal accounts are the essential route to knowing and appreciating the person
Professional is sceptical of personal stories and explanations	Professional knows the person inside out
Childhood trauma is the precursor or predictor of adult dysfunction	Childhood trauma is not predictive; it may weaken or strengthen the individual

Professional devises treatment or care plan	Focus is on aspirations of individual, family or community
Professional is the expert on service user's life	Individual, family or community are the experts
Possibilities for choice, control, commitment and personal development are limited by label/ diagnosis or condition	Possibilities for choice, control, commitment and personal development are open
Professionals' knowledge, skills and connections are the principal resources for service user	The strengths, capacities and adaptive skills of the individual, family or community are the principal resources
Support is centred on reducing the effects of symptoms and the negative effects of emotions or relationships	Support is focused on getting on with one's life, affirming and developing values and commitments, and making or finding membership in a community

Rankin (2006) identifies the following as key aspects of the strengths perspective in social care work:

▶ **Every person, family and community has strengths** (it sounds obvious, but how often do people get 'bogged down' in seeing individuals as 'difficult'?) – professionals need to suspend their disbelief about people, just as much as service users and family members may need to do so about their own abilities; the professional role is seen as one which enables people to achieve this by focusing on their strengths and resources

▶ **The concept of community is key to understanding and developing strengths** – the literature highlights dialogue, collaboration and membership of networks as key to successful strengths-based approaches

▶ **Trauma, abuse and difficulties can be hurtful, but may also be sources of challenge and opportunity** ('if it doesn't kill you, it makes you stronger') – resilience, independence and loyalty to one or more people can arise due to a painful or traumatic personal experience; people can develop great insight into their own situation

► **There are no 'upper limits' to people's abilities to grow and change**
– so we should take people's individual and collective goals seriously

► **We are most helpful to people when we work *with* them** – most
professionals will probably say that they already apply the strengths
perspective to their work, but the strengths perspective calls on the
professional to move away from the objective, concrete and tangible;
professionals have to connect with the individuals with whom they work in
a manner that recognises hope, aspirations, spirituality, identity and
belonging – this connection needs to be rooted in a true sense of equality

► **Every situation and context is full of resources and opportunities**
– the worker is required to enable the service user to recognise the talents,
resources, skills and support network which they have

▶ **People's own ideas, priorities and solutions are what we should work from** – if we don't do this, then we won't meet that person's needs effectively. Even if someone's own solution may not be what we as 'experts' think is best, it is better for the person to develop a solution for themselves, as they know themselves better than we ever will. Also, people are more likely to stick to a plan they feel belongs to them than one which feels imposed upon them by others

RESILIENCE

Resilience refers to supporting people to develop their own reservoir of skills, abilities and knowledge. Resilience is not about ignoring the real challenges people face, but it does involve acknowledging people's own resources, abilities and ways of getting through these challenges.

The resilience perspective recognises that individuals can have difficulties in one area of their life. One of the ways a person overcomes a difficulty is by drawing on other aspects of their life, either directly to problem solve or indirectly so that the person has a sense that in other areas of their life they are doing well.

WHAT DEVELOPS RESILIENCE?

Resilience is sometimes seen as a personal characteristic. However, there are steps which can help people to develop their 'resolve':

▶ Contact with other people in a similar situation

▶ Access to others who care about us in a genuine way

▶ Developing a strong personal support network

▶ Feeling that we have solved an issue before – this makes us more likely to feel able to cope next time we face something similar

▶ Praise and recognition of our achievements

▶ Acknowledgement of our strengths, uniqueness, talents and qualities

▶ Trying something new or feeling we are learning new skills

▶ A strong sense of identity, including our cultural and personal resources

▶ People seeing us as being the expert about ourselves

Note how similar these are to the key aspects of empowerment.

LISTENING AND HEARING

Empowerment relies on the development of empathic holistic relationships. **Tolan** (2003) describes this type of relationship as one where the practitioner is able to 'see the whole world as the other person sees it and is wholly accepting of that world'. The foundation of such relationships is active listening – not only through traditional listening to 'words' but also through the use of observational skills.

The following poem written by a person with learning disabilities illustrates the importance of active listening:

To work with me,
You have to listen to me
And you can't just listen with your ears.
Because it will go to your head too fast. You have to listen
with your whole body.

If you listen slow, some of what I say
Will enter your heart.

written by a **Canadian student with learning disabilities**
source unknown

The vital importance of active listening to empowerment is recognised by the **Yorkshire and Humber Empowerment Partnership** (2011:28) who state that 'We need to practise genuine listening, and not hearing what we think we want to hear.'

In fact, effective listening is very powerful in itself, as **Buscaglia** (online undated) states: 'Too often we underestimate the power of a listening ear.'

Working on the basis that social care is built on empowerment, remember that many of the foundations of empowerment are the basic skills of social care.

INFORMATION AND EMPOWERMENT

The concept of providing information as a method of empowerment is probably built on the well-known sentence first coined by Francis Bacon, a 17th century philosopher: knowledge is power.

Penhale and Parker (2008) recognise the vital importance of providing information to service users. With the rise in the use of information technology, **Matthews et al** (2011) recognise that a key part of the provision of information for service users is ensuring that people have access to information technology.

A key part of an empowerment-focused practitioner's role is recognising the importance of information in empowerment. Aspects of this are more complex than simply the provision of information. For example, **Seabury, Seabury and Garvin** (2011:130) state that:

The only power base that a client brings into the relationship is informational. The client has control over much of the information that makes up his or her situation, yet this base may be weakened when a worker enters the situation after consulting with significant others who already know the client.

The relationship between information and empowerment then should be seen as a two-way one. When thinking about providing information, consider:

▶ What information does the person want and need?

▶ Is this available in an accessible manner?

▶ What might be the best way to provide this information?

▶ Does the person have access to ICT?

When thinking about obtaining information, consider:

- ▶ What information do I need?
- ▶ Why?
- ▶ What would be the most empowering way to obtain this information?
- ▶ Does the person want to share this information?
- ▶ What do I do if they choose not to share this information?

ENABLING AND FACILITATING LEARNING

Education has long been viewed as a key element of empowerment. In the UK, this aspect of empowerment practice has largely focused on community education and developing community participation (**Yorkshire and Humber Empowerment Partnership** 2011), although in many European countries social pedagogy focuses on empowering individuals through lifelong learning.

Social pedagogy has a long history in many European countries, particularly Denmark, France, Italy, Germany and the Netherlands. The UK Government is now recognising the role of social pedagogues and showing an increasing interest in this approach in Government policy (particularly in relation to children's services). The historical roots of social pedagogy involve taking an individualised educational approach with people to support their learning. Essentially, the approach is about educating people in a way which recognises their role as active learners, so that they can take a full and active role in an inclusive society.

Empowerment is a key concept and aim in social pedagogy. Methods for achieving this include:

▶ Promoting each individual's wellbeing
▶ Holistic learning
▶ Focusing on individuals even in group settings
▶ Positive empowering and professional relationships between the professional and the person accessing services.

Whilst there are very few social pedagogues in the UK at present, it is a growing field of interest and certainly aspects of the pedagogy role can be drawn on by social care workers seeking to empower service users.

Cameron (2007) states that:

The social pedagogue works with the whole person, and supports their all-round development. Pedagogues employ theories, professional knowledge, and creative and practical skills with groups and on an individual basis. They acknowledge uncertainty and constantly review situations and decisions, in dialogue with colleagues. Human rights and participation underpin social pedagogy.

One key aspect of social pedagogy is encouraging service users to reflect on their life situation and experiences, and to see these as opportunities for learning.

The power of experiencing something positive – something that makes us happy, something we have achieved, a new skill we have learned, the caring support from someone else [...] raises our self-confidence and feeling of self-worth, so it reinforces our sense of wellbeing, of learning, of being able to form strong relationships, or of feeling empowered.
ThemPra 2009

PERSONAL COMMITMENT

The vital importance of practitioners having a personal commitment to empowerment practice is widely acknowledged.

Lum (2010) recognises that whilst empowerment requires 'social transformation on a massive scale', it must begin with each individual having a personal commitment to empowerment and to making a difference.

To work in an empowering way it is therefore vital that you reflect on your personal commitment to empowerment. How committed are you? How do you demonstrate this in your practice?

Friere (1970) stated that: 'Washing one's hands of the conflict between the powerful and the powerless means to side with the powerful, not to be neutral.'

FACILITATING USER INVOLVEMENT

Involving service users in every aspect of service provision is a vital aspect of empowerment in social care. Service users must be meaningfully involved in all aspects of the service, such as:

- ▶ Assessment and care processes (through self-assessment or co-production)
- ▶ Service provision
- ▶ Service development
- ▶ Future service planning
- ▶ Wider discussions about care services

Gallagher (2010:2) states that user involvement can be seen on two levels:

First there is the engagement of the social care worker with the client in the business of carrying out social care. Second there is the more consultative or participative understanding of engagement as the process of eliciting the views of users about what they want from social services, with the aim of listening to and responding to these views.

On a group level, many services and service providers are beginning to recognise the need to encourage service user participation and have responded to this in various ways through actions such as:

- ▶ Involving service users in management groups and service planning groups
- ▶ Involving service users in interviews, induction, staff training and education
- ▶ Setting up service user consultation groups
- ▶ User groups managing particular aspects of service delivery
- ▶ Peer reviews
- ▶ Co-production of assessments and care plan
- ▶ Surveys and focus groups
- ▶ User development of charters and standards for delivery

Research (eg **Branfield and Beresford** 2006) indicates that two activities are central to making user involvement work:

- ▶ People being able to get together to work collectively for change and mutual support
- ▶ Service users' knowledge, experience, views and ideas being listened to and valued

This leaves us with the chicken and egg question – user involvement is empowering, but how do we empower people so that they can effectively engage in consultation? Which comes first? Again, this demonstrates the complexity of empowerment.

People think the only thing we know is how to moan. But they are not listening. We know what needs changing, what works and what doesn't work. We know this because we live it 24/7, 52 weeks a year with no days off.
Service user in Branfield and Beresford 2006

COMMENTS AND COMPLAINTS PROCEDURES

Comments and complaints procedures are an essential aspect of giving service users a voice and working towards empowerment.

An effective complaints procedure is crucial for service users, but it can also be helpful for practitioners in that an effective complaints procedure can:

- Bring attention to lack of resources
- Emphasise the need for a high quality service provision
- Identify areas of poor practice
- Support staff to develop their practice
- Clarify misunderstandings
- Ensure that service users' concerns are appropriately directed rather than creating conflict within the professional relationship
- Challenge the status quo
- Test and improve systems and processes

It is therefore important that social care professionals do not view complaints procedures negatively or as a threat. A good quality complaints procedure is a positive attribute to a service. It will encourage recipients of the service to participate more in it and have more control over the services they receive.

However, service users often experience problems in making use of complaints procedures. Research by **Finnegan and Clarke** in 2005 identified that:

▶ 76% of staff agreed or strongly agreed with the statement that 'very few service users use the formal complaints procedure'

▶ 82% agreed with the statement that service users 'do not understand the process'

▶ 76% agreed with the statement 'they do not understand their rights'

Comments from staff involved in this research about the lack of use of complaints procedures included the following:

Service users just don't like complaining. I can see why they wouldn't because I don't think I would feel at ease doing that if I was them. I'd be worried about being seen as a troublemaker I suppose, and you might be worried about how you might get treated afterwards.

My worry is that they complain less and less because nothing is ever done …

The service users really do not feel that they can complain against someone who has power over their lives. It stays within the house and is not properly recorded or followed-up.

I know that every time there is an incident or complaint, everything should be written down but that is never the case.

Finnegan and Clarke 2005

PRACTICE EXAMPLE

Marian is 88 and lives in a care home. For some years she and her family have felt that the activities on offer are not frequent or interesting enough. Marian chooses to make a complaint with the support of her daughter, Sue. She asks a worker how she can do this and they say they do not know. Marian and Sue see the manager, who tells her that the complaint will be looked into, but two weeks later, no one has got back to them.

▶ Why are services worried about people making complaints?

▶ Why are service users often reluctant to complain?

▶ What is your service's policy on complaints?

▶ How are service users made aware of it?

▶ How would someone like Marian receive feedback on their complaint in your service?

▶ How do complaints and feedback empower people?

PERSONALISATION AND EMPOWERMENT

Personalisation is a key component of contemporary social care practice. Stressed in current Government policy, it is being implemented across a changing landscape and is often referred to in transformational terms.

The use of the word personalisation is currently more established in England, whereas in the three other nations of the UK, person-centred care is a more common term. The idea of personalisation encompasses the values of person-centred care in ensuring that the care people receive is right for each individual, as opposed to a 'one size fits all' approach to services. However, the personalisation of services is much broader, as it includes empowering individuals with budgets to control their own services far more and changing the whole way in which services are commissioned, provided and constructed to meet different people's specific needs.

Arguments for personalisation include references to it being a key method of empowerment in contemporary social care. For example, **Alzheimer Scotland** (2011) assert that personalisation empowers individuals and families to direct their own services and their own lives.

The idea is therefore that personalised care, individual budgets and self-directed support are all interlinked as concepts which should ensure that the service user is empowered to manage their own care, as opposed to being a passive recipient of it.

DIRECT PAYMENTS AND PERSONAL BUDGETS

One practical application of the personalisation agenda is the development of personal budgets and direct payments.

Direct payments are available to people who have been assessed as eligible for free social care by their local authority. The payments are given to the individual (or someone acting on their behalf) so that they can arrange and buy their own care rather than use traditional services provided by the local authority.

Personal budgets are based on personal need and they can be paid directly to the service user or managed by someone else on their behalf. Personal budgets may be taken as direct payments. Direct payments arguably represent one of the most practical tools for empowerment currently available in social care practice.

EMPOWERMENT AND ANTI-OPPRESSIVE PRACTICE

According to **Hepworth et al** (2010:414) empowerment 'assumes that issues of power (and powerlessness) are inextricably linked to the experiences of oppression'.

The word oppression has its roots in Latin. It comes from the word opprimere which means 'to press on' or 'press against'. As such, it suggests being pressed on and flattened – not being allowed to grow and develop. Looking at oppression in this way gives a very visual image of what it is like to be oppressed.

Anti-oppressive practice seeks both to identify and challenge the mechanisms of oppression in order to empower individuals and groups. For example, **Singh and Cowden** (2009) argue that social care workers should 'not succumb to power, but engage in uncovering, confronting and resisting power'.

Identifying oppression: enabling people to recognise the way in which they are oppressed is a key aspect of empowerment practice. **Gardner** (2011) suggests that practitioners must encourage service users to understand the connections between their own circumstances and the broader socio-political context in which they exist.

Challenging oppression: seeking to challenge oppression is also a key aspect of empowerment – **Zastrow** (2010:52) states that: 'Empowerment focused practitioners seek a more equitable distribution of resources and power among the various groups in society.'

Working in an anti-oppressive way, and recognising and challenging oppression is an essential aspect of empowerment.

ENCOURAGING HOPEFULNESS

The importance of people retaining a sense of hope has long been recognised as vital in mental health. The recovery model, for example, refers to the importance of the service user having someone who will hold a 'candle of hope'. People who achieve 'recovery' relate the importance of having people around them who continue to hope and convey a sense of confidence that recovery will eventually occur.

There are lots of changes in lifestyle that a service user may express a commitment to address. When the service user does not achieve their own goal, then those working with them need to be respectful. The service user may not even be honest to staff about failing to achieve their goal. Such honesty could make the service user feel stripped of all dignity (they have failed again). Good workers will enable a service user to have a sense of their dignity whilst maintaining an honest dialogue.

In order to avoid situations where staff members' hopefulness appears superficial, it may be more helpful to describe the professional quality as realistic optimism. The service user could well find any planned change demanding, but change is possible.

Every journey begins with a single step.
   McKinnon 1998

POWER AND EMPOWERMENT

APPRECIATING THE SMALL THINGS

Social care workers often deal with issues that are entrenched over a number of years and generally involve a range of complex factors. It can be easy to lose sight of achievements and positive change within this. Sometimes people's needs and difficulties are so significant that small achievements are not recognised. Workers can develop a cynical approach, which may be communicated, albeit unconsciously, to service users.

It is important for social care workers to maintain a positive attitude to practice. Part of this will involve recognising that complex and difficult situations will not change overnight.

Practitioners need to notice and appreciate every step that is taken and every positive in the work they do; they also need to encourage service users to recognise even small positive changes.

PRACTICE EXAMPLE

Zaniya is a worker in a drug and alcohol service. She is working with several individuals, including those who have been users of the service for several years. Zaniya has observed colleagues saying that some individuals are not committed to making changes, as they keep going back into substance use, miss appointments and do not stick to agreed programmes for harm reduction. Zaniya hears one of her colleagues say that 'there's no point' offering one service user another appointment as 'he'll never change'. She is concerned that this is not the same as her view of the person and that the worker is being too pessimistic.

▶   What are Zaniya's options in this situation?
▶   What are the possible implications if she takes certain actions?
▶   What would *you* do or say in this situation?
▶   How can Zaniya maintain hopefulness and empower the service user?

BREAKING THE VICIOUS CYCLE

The cognitive model of depression (**Beck et al** 1979) demonstrates the importance of hope in breaking the 'vicious cycle' of this illness. Beck's model is often likened to the process of learned helplessness which demonstrates the fact that hope and positivity can assist in empowerment.

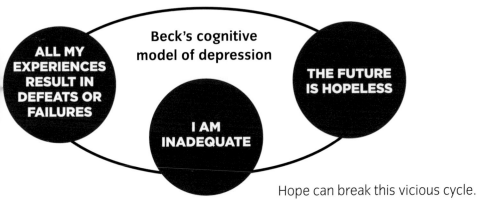

Beck's cognitive model of depression

ALL MY EXPERIENCES RESULT IN DEFEATS OR FAILURES

I AM INADEQUATE

THE FUTURE IS HOPELESS

Hope can break this vicious cycle.

Beck's cognitive model of depression

▶ The future is hopeless

▶ I am inadequate

▶ All my experiences result in defeats or failures

Hope can break this vicious cycle.

The concept of 'Hopeful Social Care Practice' has been developed in Australia, where hope has been identified as a central feature in working with people with physical illness, acquired physical disabilities, medical conditions and mental health problems (**Darlington and Bland** 1999).

Hopeful social care practice recognises the following crucial elements of hope (**Miller and Powers** 1988:8):

- Mutuality affiliation – having a sense of belonging
- Sense of the possible – seeing things as possible
- Avoidance of absolutising – not imposing rigid conditions on 'hoped for' situations
- Anticipation – looking forward to a positive future
- Achieving goals
- Psychological wellbeing and coping
- Sense of freedom
- Reality-surveillance optimism – searching for clues that confirm maintaining hope is feasible
- Mental and physical activation – maintaining activity to maintain hope

Although 'hopeful practice' is not a phrase widely used in social care in the UK, the growth of interest in spirituality in the field is closely related.

It would be useful for social care workers in the UK to consider the development of hopeful practice, especially in the current climate. Not least because, as **Stanford** (2011) asserts, hopeful practice can assist social care professionals who in recent times are struggling to maintain their professional focus and values in their day-to-day practice.

POWER AND EMPOWERMENT

DEVELOPING POSITIVE ATTITUDE AND PRACTICES

It is widely accepted that attitude impacts on emotions. Positive attitudes have a positive impact on emotional wellbeing and a positive effect on feelings of personal empowerment, thus developing the 'power within'.

A whole industry has built itself up around the power of positive thinking. However, many workers often underestimate the importance of positive thinking in empowerment.

Henry Ford is attributed with saying: 'If you think you can or you think you can't … You're right!'

TOP TIPS FOR POSITIVE THINKING

Social care professionals work in very difficult situations. This can mean they find positive thinking more difficult. In a climate of scarce resources many workers often find themselves having to focus on the negatives at work. The worst possible picture has to be painted simply to obtain basic services or to justify any form of intervention. So, whilst some of the following tips might sound very trite, do think about them carefully. You can assist service users to develop positive thinking, and it wouldn't do any harm for practitioners to develop their own positive thinking.

▶ Smile regularly – develop your sense of humour
▶ List the positives in your life – think about everything good
▶ List the negatives – don't dwell on what they are but rather think about which ones you can change immediately, which ones you can change in the longer term, and accept those things which you cannot change
▶ Try positive visualisation

- ▶ Let go of any negative feelings you have towards someone else – the negative thoughts hurt you more than anyone else
- ▶ Surround yourself with positivity – listen to positive music, watch positive films, look at positive images; the impact of the senses on your mood and thought processes cannot be underestimated
- ▶ Maintain a solution-focused approach
- ▶ Consider approaches which have a positive view, such as strengths perspectives
- ▶ Look for the opportunities in every difficulty

Social care can create a negative thinking pattern. We actively need to consider how to support service users in developing and maintaining positive thinking.

HELPING SERVICE USERS TO DEVELOP RESOURCES

Empowerment involves supporting people to develop a range of personal resources including:

Confidence
Service users need to have confidence which relates closely to 'power within'.

Confidence building can be a difficult and slow task. Ways to enhance confidence can include:

▶ Joining with others who have had similar experiences and who have successfully changed their life positively
▶ Individuals choosing an aspect of their life they want to change so there is a good chance of this being achieved
▶ Encouraging a person to have a supporter or advocate present when they raise an issue of concern to them

A 'voice'

When a service user expresses something about their own life, practitioners and services should listen. Sometimes it can be difficult to listen to the service user's voice because there is so much 'background noise' (or so many other voices). People can be so poor at listening effectively to a service user that having a voice may need to involve the person having an advocate.

Problem-solving approach

The service user will need to recognise that practical difficulties could arise in seeking to change their own life in the way they would like to. To achieve their goal, they will need to adopt a problem-solving or solution-focused attitude.

Personal resources

As discussed, supporting service users to develop their personal resolve and maintain a hopeful outlook is an important aspect of empowerment.

EMPOWERMENT AND THE DIGNITY OF RISK

One of the key aspects of empowering people is to enable and support them to take risks and make informed choices.

It sounds obvious, but:

▶ Services have often in the past been too protective of people
▶ Services have always sought to minimise or eliminate any risk of harm (emotional or physical harm)
▶ The attempt to eliminate all risk undermines people's dignity and inhibits opportunities for personal development and growth
▶ Care environments that reduce risk as much as possible result in impoverished environments
▶ Good risk assessments balance people's rights with consideration of risk and consequences

The notion that one has options from which to choose is often more important than the particular option one initially selects.

Anthony 2000

The aim should be for services to support people to take measured risks and to choose for themselves, where possible, how to live their own lives. As people are supported to develop and extend their skills, the risks associated should be evaluated to see if the person can extend their level of independence.

Risk-taking is an integral part of daily life and is a significant route to supporting service users to maintain a sense of achievement and fulfilment. If it is handled in a planned and conscious way, it can be a great springboard for all. We all take risks every time we step out of the front door, get in or drive a car, light a cigarette (if we smoke), drink alcohol, and so on, so why do services sometimes prevent their users from having the same choices?

The idea that there is dignity in risk is sometimes referred to as the 'right to failure'. By taking away all risks from people, they can be denied the right to self-determination – that is, to decide for themselves how they want to live their life, even if the choices they make may not always be the 'best' ones.

Empowering people to take risks is not just about 'allowing' or 'permitting' actions to occur. It involves:

▶   Examination of one's own values to the action the person wants to take (what is your view on smoking?; what about people's sexual preferences?, etc)
▶   Discussion about the whole range of choices which are available to the person, as well as the possible consequences (both positive and negative) of making certain choices
▶   Explaining to others why you are doing this, as other people may be challenged by empowerment when it actually happens in this way

▶ Continuing to support the person, even if they make the choice you may not have expected, and even (or maybe especially) if they experience those negative consequences

The governing principle behind good approaches to risk is that people have the right to live their lives to the full as long as that does not stop others from doing the same.

Department of Health 2008

ADVOCACY

Advocacy is a widely accepted principle of good practice. In many ways, though it now has a significant history within services, advocacy is often implemented in a half-hearted way with a lack of real commitment from services and staff teams.

Essentially, there are two different forms of advocacy.

Self-advocacy

This is where the individual refines the skills they already have to speak for themselves. Often self-advocates join together to form groups, both to gain a sense of personal support and to have more of an impact on the services they receive.

Self-advocacy is about enabling and empowering people to act on their own behalf. There is no doubt that this is a powerful way of helping people achieve independence, although it might not be feasible for all service users. Often assertiveness training is needed in order to help people raise their confidence and sense of self-worth, and to teach the skills necessary to make other people listen.

Many services now have self-advocacy groups. If staff limit their understanding of self-advocacy to the people who are members of such groups and to the topics discussed in the group, they misunderstand the aim of the whole advocacy movement. People should be listened to as they express their views and make decisions about their own life and the services they receive on a day-to-day basis.

It is the failure of staff and services to listen to people as a matter of course that has resulted in the rise of the self-advocacy movement.

Citizen advocacy or professional advocacy

This is also known as independent advocacy. This is where an individual enters into a partnership with a service user with the intention to express clearly what the person is communicating. Citizen advocates are usually volunteers (unpaid). However, advocates are increasingly employed by advocacy services – hence the term professional advocacy.

It is not the job of the citizen advocate (or professional advocate) to say what they think is best for the person they have got to know. Their task is to convey what the service user is trying to say even if they disagree with what the person is saying. If the person could advocate for themselves, then the citizen advocate would not be needed, so it is vital that people acting as advocates for others do so with this in mind.

Independent advocacy is important because most service users find themselves compromised in one way or another in terms of expressing their own views:

There is a strong power imbalance in favour of the authorities
Individuals may be lacking in confidence
They may not have the verbal or other communication skills to express clearly their own meaning
Their families may not agree with their own views and may put pressure on the person

An advocate can help someone work out exactly what they want, if necessary, and then challenge services on that person's behalf.

Sometimes confusion reigns as to who can be an advocate. Strictly speaking, any person working for an organisation providing services or goods to an individual cannot act as that person's advocate. This is because an employee unavoidably has competing loyalties. Also, some of us find it hard not to impose what we think is best for the service user and would genuinely struggle to present the latter's own views as paramount. We need to recognise this and allow someone else to take on that role on behalf of the service user.

THE LIMITS OF ADVOCACY

One of the central dilemmas of advocacy has been that a citizen advocate or professional advocate requires the service user to express their view, thus raising two questions:

Why does that person need an advocate?
Service users who can express themselves may need an advocate either for reasons of moral support or because services haven't listened to them up to now.

What about service users who cannot express themselves clearly?

Some advocates feel that they can identify what a person is seeking to communicate even if they have no clear language. The advocate will act in accordance with the idea of 'non-instructed advocacy'. They will observe the service user and try and gauge from the person's facial expression, body language and any vocal sounds or simple words what they like and dislike. Sometimes the advocate will draw information from people who know the service user well (family members or direct care staff) and this will be used to create as full a picture as possible. By spending time with the service user and observing them (this is sometimes called a 'watching brief'), the advocate hopes to be able to get to a position where they feel they can express something of the service user's viewpoint.

Some vulnerable people, who don't have clear communication skills, can still be left almost completely voiceless.

PRACTICE EXAMPLE

Sean is 24 and has autism. He attends a day centre once a week and enjoys several activities such as chess, swimming and card games. A worker notices that Sean and another user of the centre are beginning to form a close bond and talks to Sean's family about this to see if they would like to make other opportunities for Sean to develop this relationship away from the centre. Sean's mother is unhappy that this relationship could potentially be promoted by the centre, as she feels that Sean is not ready or able to have emotional or sexual relationships. She says she is considering making a complaint and possibly withdrawing Sean from attending the service.

▶ What could a worker do to enable Sean's own views to be explored or to ensure he can access advocacy?

▶ What implications could this have, and how could these be worked through?

▶ What assumptions have been made in this situation?

CRITICALLY REFLECTIVE PRACTICE

Jan Fook is perhaps the most well-known contemporary writer on reflective practice in social care work and her writings on the subject (eg 2002) emphasise the vital importance of the practitioner reflecting on power dynamics and their implications. Fook's model is essentially based on a three-step process.

1   Telling the narrative
2   Deconstructing the situation
3   Reconstructing the situation

Telling the narrative

Effectively, this is where the practitioner is describing the practice and what was occurring in the situation chosen as the critical incident.

Deconstructing the situation

This is essentially a stage of reflective questioning by exploring the practice. Fook focuses on exploring issues of power and how power is constructed.

Reconstructing the situation

This is the stage of planning future practice and putting the plans into action (Fook refers to redeveloping practice). Again, she stresses paying particular attention to power relationships and how power structures and relationships can be changed to be more emancipatory.

Reflecting on your use of power and on your ability to apply empowerment in practice is vital. Fook's model can be helpful in reminding practitioners to reflect on power. In many ways reflective practice is about a process of dynamic questioning; considering the following questions might assist you in developing your reflection on empowerment:

REFLECTING ON POWER

Definitions

▷ *How do you define power?*
▷ *How do you define empowerment?*
▷ *Which other definitions of power and empowerment do you find useful? Why?*

Ongoing development of your practice

▷ *What opportunities can I take to keep on learning about power and empowerment?*
▷ *In what ways can I keep these issues on my agenda and that of my colleagues?*
▷ *Do I use supervision effectively to reflect on power?*
▷ *Who and what can help me to keep developing?*

Considering service users' situations

▷ *In what ways was the service user powerful?*
▷ *In what ways were they disempowered?*
▷ *How did they feel about me coming into their life?*
▷ *How would I feel if our roles were reversed?*
▷ *How did I communicate their expertise on their own needs, what their rights are and what options they have?*
▷ *Did we both understand these things in the same way?*
▷ *How did I empower the person?*
▷ *Did I disempower them in any way? How? Why?*

General practice

> *What aspects of my practice are empowering?*
> *What aspects of my practice are disempowering?*
> *How do I use the various components of empowerment?*
> *What aspects of empowerment do I find most challenging? Why?*
> *How do I express my personal commitment to empowerment?*

Adopting a critically reflective approach to practice in general can assist in empowerment, particularly as it highlights power differentials and enables practitioners to reconstruct power. It is also important to adopt a reflective approach to empowerment, which involves practitioners exploring a range of questions.

EMPOWERMENT: CAKE OR SPIDER'S WEB?

We have referred to the value of considering empowerment in terms of its key ingredients. It is important to recognise, though, that there are dangers to this approach and breaking theories down into component parts can lead to mechanistic practice.

One of the dangers in breaking empowerment down is that whenever a practitioner does one of the things we have discussed, they may claim to have 'empowered' a service user. In maintaining the recipe analogy, empowerment could be compared to a complex multi-layered cake. The cake cannot be made without all (or at least most) of the ingredients.

Whilst it can be useful to consider the 'ingredients' when looking at what specific practical actions social care workers can take, it is vital to remember that empowerment is not the icing on the cake – it's the cake!

Throughout this section of the Pocket Guide it is clear that there are links between the different components we have highlighted. In many ways, a visual representation of empowerment could look like a spider's web with connections between the many different elements.

Regular reference is made to 'networks of power' and the construction of power. Picturing a spider's web and how it is constructed around a range of 'networks' provides a useful visual image of empowerment. In constructing webs, spiders often find the most difficult thread is the first and until a number of threads are in place, the web is vulnerable to being blown away – just like empowerment!

EMPOWERMENT: THE NEVER-ENDING JOURNEY?

The **Yorkshire and Humber Empowerment Partnership** (2011) describe empowerment as a journey. They make the point that we are all at different stages on the journey towards empowerment.

Generally, when we are going on a journey, we plan to reach a particular destination. However, would it be more appropriate to view empowerment as a never-ending journey? Those practitioners who claimed to have empowered people generally have a very simplistic view of empowerment.

So we end this Pocket Guide almost where we started this section; maybe, as a never-ending journey, empowerment is an aspirational rather than an achievable goal in contemporary social care work. However, there are approaches we can use and routes we can take which will make the journey a more useful and empowering one.

See the empowerment journey as one to be enjoyed and shared with the service user. There may be times when you take the driving seat for various reasons but, on the whole, the idea of empowerment is that the service user should be in the driving seat – or at the very least, directing the journey.

REFERENCES

Alzheimer Scotland (2011) *Let's Get Personal: Personalisation and Dementia*. Available online at www.alzscot.org/pages/policy/report-personalisation-and-dementia.htm. Accessed 29.4.11

Anthony, W (2000) 'A Recovery Oriented Service System: Setting Some System Level Standards' in *Psychiatric Rehabilitation Journal*, 24(2) pp159–168

Association of Directors of Social Services (2005) *Safeguarding Adults: A National Framework of Standards for Good Practice and Outcomes in Adult Protection Work*. (London) ADSS

Bar-On, A (2002) 'Restoring Power to Social Work Practice' in *British Journal of Social Work*, 32(8) pp997–1014

Barker, R L (2009) *The Social Work Dictionary*. (5th edition) (Washington) NASW Press

Beck, A T, Rush, A J, Shaw, B F and Emery, G (1979) *Cognitive Therapy of Depression*. (New York) Guildford

Bernhagen, P (2003) 'Power: making sense of an elusive concept' in *Journal of Post Graduate Research*, 2 pp62–82

Betts Adams, K, Matto, H C and LeCroy, C W (2009) *Limitations of evidence-based practice for social work education: unpacking the complexity.* Available online at http://findarticles.com/p/articles/mi_hb3060/is_2_45/ai_n35624095/pg_9. Accessed 29.9.11

Branfield, F and Beresford, P (2006) *Making user involvement work: supporting service user networking and knowledge.* Joseph Rowntree Foundation. Available online at http://www.jrf.org.uk/publications/making-user-involvement-work-supporting-service-user-networking-and-knowledge. Accessed 13.10.11

Buscaglia, L F (1972) *Love.* (New York) Fawcett

Cameron, C (2007) *Social Pedagogy and the Children's Workforce.* Available online at www.communitycare.co.uk/Articles/2007/08/08/105392/social_pedagogy_and_the_childrens_workforce.htm. Accessed 19.1.10

Chanan, G and Miller, C (2010) *The Big Society: How It Could Work.* (London) PACES

Clarke, J, Gewirtz, S and McLaughlin, E (eds) (2000) *New Managerialism, New Welfare*. (London) Sage

Commission for Social Care Inspection (2008) *Safeguarding adults: a study of the effectiveness of arrangements to safeguard adults from abuse*. (London) CSCI

Cooper, B (2011) 'Criticality and Reflexivity: Best Practice in Uncertain Environments' in **Seden, J, Matthews, S, McCormick, M, and Morgan, A** (eds) *Professional Development in Social Work: Complex Issues in Practice*. (Oxon) Routledge

Croft, S and Beresford, P (1992) 'The Politics of Participation' in *Critical Social Policy*, 35, pp20–44

Darlington, Y and Bland, R (1999) 'Strategies for Encouraging and Maintaining Hope Among People Living with Serious Mental Illness' in *Australian Social Work*, 52, pp17–24

Department of Health (2008) *Transforming Adult Social Care*. (London) The Stationery Office

Department of Health (2009) *Written Ministerial Statement. Government Response to the Consultation on Safeguarding Adults: the Review of the No Secrets Guidance*. Available online at http://webarchive. nationalarchives.gov.uk/+/www.dh.gov.uk/en/Consultations/ Responsestoconsultations/DH_111286. Accessed 1.10.11

Dominelli, L (2002) *Anti-Oppressive Social Work Theory and Practice*. (Basingstoke) Palgrave Macmillan

Duluth Model (2011) *Home of the Duluth Model*. Available online at www. theduluthmodel.org. Accessed 4.10.11

Ewart, B and Hindley, A (2011) 'Is the time right for a rebirth of true community development?' in **Yorkshire and Humber Empowerment Partnership** (2011) *Empowerment: Reflections from Yorkshire and Humber*. Available online at www.yhep.org.uk. Accessed 29.9.11

Finnegan, P and Clarke, S (2005) *One Law for All? The Impact of the Human Rights Act on People with Learning Difficulties*. (London) Values into Action

Fook, J (2002) *Social Work: Critical Theory and Practice.* (London) Sage

Foucault, M (1977) *Discipline and Punish: The Birth of the Prison.* (London) Tavistock

Friere, P (1970) *Pedagogy of the Oppressed.* (New York) Herder and Herder

French, J and Raven, B H (1959) 'The bases of social power' in **Cartwright, D** (ed) *Studies in Social Power.* pp150–167. (Ann Arbor) Institute for Social Research

Gallagher, M (2010) *Engaging with Involuntary service users in social work.* Available online at http://www.socialwork.ed.ac.uk/__data/assets/pdf_file/0011/37874/engaging_briefing.pdf. Accessed 13.10.11

Gardner, A (2011) *Personalisation in Social Work.* (Exeter) Learning Matters

Hepworth, D H, Rooney, R H, Dewberry Rooney, G, Strom-Gottfried, K and Larsen, J A (2010) *Direct Social Work Practice: Theory and Skills.* (Belmont) Cengage Learning

Higham, P (2005) *What is important about social work and social care?* Available online at www.ssrg.org.uk/assembly/files/patriciahigham.pdf. Accessed 26.10.09

Hinson, S and Healey, R (2003) *Building Political Power. Prepared for the State Strategies Fund Convening*. Grassroots Policy Project

Inner London Probation Service (1993) *Working with Difference: A Positive and Practical Guide to Anti-Discriminatory Practice Teaching*. (London) Inner London Probation Service

International Federation of Social Workers (2011) *The Social Impact of the Financial Crisis: Project Papers*. Presented at IFSW Symposium. ENSACT Conference, Brussels, 10–13 April 2011

Just Associates (2006) *Making Change Happen: Power. Concepts for Revisioning Power for Justice, Equality and Peace*. (Washington) Just Associates

Kennedy, R F Available online at http://www.wisdomword.info/robert-f-kennedy-2/. Accessed 12.1.11

Kreisberg, S (1992) *Transforming Power: Domination, Empowerment and Education*. (Albany) State University of New York Press

Livestrong.com (2011) *Accepting Powerlessness*.
Available online at www.livestrong.com/article/14716_accepting_powerlessness. Accessed 18.6.11

Lopez, J (2011) *Contemporary Sociological Theories*. Available online at http://ssms.socialsciences.uottawa.ca/vfs/.horde/offre_cours/syllabus/00028710205_SOC7110A.pdf. Accessed 1.8.11

Lukes, S (1986) (ed) *Power*. (Oxford) Basil Blackwell

Lukes, S (2004) *Power: A Radical View*. (2nd edition) Palgrave Macmillan

Lum, D (2010) *Culturally Competent Practice: A Framework for Understanding Diverse Groups and Justice Issues*. (Belmont) Brooks/Cole

Maclean, S and Harrison, R (2010) *Social Care: The Common Knowledge Base: A Pic 'n' Mix Guide*. (Rugeley) Kirwin Maclean Associates Ltd

Matthews, S, McCormick, M and Morgan, A (2011) (eds) *Professional Development in Social Work: Complex Issues in Practice*. (Abingdon) Routledge

McKinnon, K D (1998) *Coping with Caring: the Dangers of Chronic Stress and Burnout*. Available online at http://www.charityvillage.com/cv/research/rpersdv1.html. Accessed 30.12.10

Miller, J F and Powers, M J (1988) 'Development of an Instrument to Measure Hope' in *Nursing Research*, vol 37(1), pp6–10

Mooney, A, Thomas, L, Wareing, S, Stillwell Peccei, J, LaBelle, S, Henriksen, B E, Eppler, E, Irwin, A, Pichler, P, Preece, S and Soden, S (2011) *Language, Society and Power: An Introduction*. (3rd edition) (Oxon) Routledge

Morgenthau, H J (1978) *Politics among Nations: The Struggle for Power and Peace*. (5th edition) (New York) Knopf

Munro, E (2011) *The Munro Review of Child Protection: Final Report A Child-Centred System*. Available online at https://www.education.gov.uk/publications/eOrderingDownload/Munro-Review.pdf. Accessed 4.2.12

NSPCC (2011) *Defining Child Abuse*. Available online at http://www.nspcc.org.uk/ Inform/cpsu/helpandadvice/organisations/defining/definingchildabuse_ wda60692.html. Accessed 1.10.11

Nye, J S (2004) *Soft Power: The Means to Success in World Politics*. (New York) Public Affairs

Penhale, B and Parker, J (2008) *Working with Vulnerable Adults*. (Abingdon) Routledge

Rankin, P (2006) *Exploring and Describing the Strength/Empowerment Perspective in Social Work*. Available online at http://www.bemidjistate. edu/academics/publications/social_work_journal/issue14/articles/rankin. htm. Accessed 7.10.11

Robbins, S P, Chartterjee, P and Canda, E R (1998) *Contemporary Human Behaviour Theory*. (Boston) Allyn and Bacon

Rodgers, J (2003) *Reason, Conflict and Power: Modern Political and Social Thought from 1688 to the Present*. (Oxford) University Press of America

Saleeby, D (1996) 'The Strengths Perspective in Social Work Practice: Extensions and Cautions' in *Social Work*, vol 41, pp296–305

Scottish Government (2005) *The Role of the Social Worker in the 21st Century: A Literature Review*. (Edinburgh) Scottish Government

Seabury, B, Seabury, B and Garvin, C D (2011) *Foundations of Interpersonal Practice in Social Work: Promoting Competence in Generalist Practice*. (London) Sage

Self Esteem Experts Building Self Esteem. Available online at http://www.self-esteem-experts.com/self-esteem-building-activities-blog.html. Accessed 22.3.11

Shivers, J S (2001) *Leadership and Groups in Recreational Service*. (Cranbury) Rosemont Publishing

Singh, G and Cowden, S (2009) 'Social Worker as Intellectual' in *European Journal of Social Work*, 12(2), pp479–493

Smith, R (2010) *Social Work, Risk, Power*. Sociological Research online. Available online at http://www.socresonline.org.uk/15/1/4.html. Accessed 28.4.11

Social Platform (2010) *Briefing Number 33: Annual Theme 2010 on Care.* (Brussels) Social Platform

Stanford, S N (2011) 'Constructing Moral Responses to Risk: A Framework for Hopeful Social Work Practice' in *British Journal of Social Work*, 41(8) pp1514–1531

ThemPra Social Pedagogy Community Interest Society (2009) *Social Pedagogy: Theory Meets Practice.* Available online at www.socialpedagogy.co.uk/concepts.htm. Accessed 19.1.10

Thompson, N (2001) 'Anti-discriminatory practice' in **Davies, M** (ed) *The Blackwell Companion to Social Work* (2nd edition) (Oxford) Blackwell Publishing

Tolan, J (2003) *Skills in Person-Centred Counselling and Psychotherapy.* (London) Sage

Tuitt, W (2010) *Power and Policy: Lessons for Leaders in Government and Business.* (California) Praeger

Veneklasen, L and Miller, V (2002, reprinted 2007) *A New Weave of Power, People and Politics: the Action Guide for Advocacy and Citizen Participation*. (Oklahoma) World Neighbours

Walker, S and Beckett, C (2003) *Social Work Assessment and Intervention*. (2nd edition) (Lyme Regis) Russell House Publishing

Warrin, B (2010) 'Safeguarding Adults in Cornwall' in *The Journal of Adult Protection*, 12 (2), pp39–42

White, C, Holland, D, Marsland, D and Oakes, O (2003) 'The identification of environments and cultures that promote the abuse of people with intellectual disabilities. A review of the literature' in *Journal of Applied Research in Intellectual Disabilities*, 16, pp1–9

Williamson, M (1992) *Our Greatest Fear*. Available online at http://explorersfoundation.org/glyphery/122_html. Accessed 22.3.11

Yorkshire and Humber Empowerment Partnership (2011)
Empowerment: Reflections from Yorkshire and Humber. Available online at www.yhep.org.uk. Accessed 29.9.11

Zastrow, C (2010) *Introduction to Social Work and Social Welfare: Empowering People* (10th edition) (Belmont) Cengage Learning

City & Guilds is the UK's leading provider of vocational qualifications, offering over 500 awards across a wide range of industries, and progressing from entry level to the highest levels of professional achievement. With over 8,500 centres in 100 countries, City & Guilds is recognised by employers worldwide.

Publications

For information about, or to order support materials, contact the Publishing department on +44 (0)20 7294 4113 or learningmaterials@cityandguilds.com. More information about the materials is available at www.cityandguilds.com/publications. For further copies of this Pocket Guide, or other qualification documentation, contact our Publication Sales department on +44 (0)20 7294 2850 or by fax +44 (0)20 7294 3387.

Every effort has been made to ensure that the information contained in this publication is true and correct at the time of going to press. However, City & Guilds' products and services are subject to continuous development and improvement and the right is reserved to change products and services from time to time. City & Guilds cannot accept liability for loss or damage arising from the use of information in this publication.